# Table of Contents

1. I Feel Exhausted Today
2. I Don't Feel Confident About My Weight
3. Struggling With Not Feeling Like I am Enough
4. Maybe I Could Have Handled The Situation Better
5. Stressful Workplace
6. Mourning The Loss of A Loved One
7. Fear and Anxiety
8. Breaking Up With A Significant Other
9. I Am Heartbroken
10. I Am Afraid to Make Mistakes
11. Struggling With Diet Regimen
12. Challenging Financial Situation
13. I Disappointed Someone
14. Someone Disappointed Me
15. I Feel The Need To Apologize
16. I Didn't Receive an Apology
17. My Mental Health Feels Challenged At Times
18. I Feel Discouraged Because I Am Not Married
19. I Feel Discouraged Because I Don't Have Children
20. I Feel Lonely
21. I Miss My Family
22. Sometimes I Don't Feel Attractive
23. I Don't Feel Understood

# Table of Contents

24. Sometimes It's Challenging For Me To Concentrate
25. Self Motivation
26. Self Love
27. Holding Myself Accountable
28. Overeating
29. Remaining Humble
30. Difficult Childhood
31. Perfectionalism
32. Afraid of Commitment
33. Self Control
34. I Am Enough
35. Validation
36. Responsibility For Actions
37. Hurt Feelings
38. Performance
39. Farewell Stinking Thinking
40. Goodby Self Sabotage
41. Taking Care Of Me
42. Feeling Devalued
43. Unappreciated
44. Thankful
45. Blessed
46. Betrayal
47. Losing A Best Friend
48. Parenting Is A Joyful Journey
49. Parenting Is Challenging
50. I Will Be Successful

# I Feel Exhausted Today

I am resilent, and each breath I take fills me with new energy. My body is strong and my mind is capable. I choose to focus on what I can accomplish, and with each small step I move closer to my goals. Today's exhaustion is just a temporary state, and I am capable of overcoming it. I am deserving of rest and rejuvenation, and I trust that I have the strength to face any challenge. I am resilient, I am powerful, and I am in control of my well-being.

# I Don't Feel Confident About My Weight

I am resilient, and each breath I take fills me with new energy. My body is strong, and my mind is capable. I choose to focus on what I can accomplish, and with each small step, I move closer to my goals. Today's exhaustion is just a temporary state, and I am capapble of overcoming it. I am deserving of rest and rejuvenation, and I trust that I have the strength to face any challenge. I am resilient, I am powerful, and I am in control of my well-being.

# I am Struggling With Not Feeling Like I am Enough

I am enough just as I am. My worth is not determined by external validation or comparison. I bring unique qualities, talents, and love to the world. I embrace my imperfections, for they are a part of my beautiful journey. Today, I release the need for perfection and accept myself with kindness. I am worthy of love, success, and happiness. I acknowledge my strengths and am open to growth. Each day, I am becoming a better version of myself. I am deserving of all good things life has to offer, and I am enough.

# Maybe I Could Have Handled The Situation Better

I am human, and I acknowledge that I may not always handle situations perfectly. Today's experience is an opportunity for growth, not a measure of my worth. I choose to learn from this situation with compasssion for myself. I recognize that mistakes are a natural part of life, and they provide valuable lessions. I forgive myself for any perceived shortcomings and trust that I am evolving into a wiser and more resilient person. I am committed to continuous improvement, and each moment is a chance for me to respond with grace and wisdom. I am learning, growing, and becoming a better version of myself every day.

# My Workplace Was Stressful Today

Today may have been challenging, but I am resilient and capable. I acknowledge the stress I faced, and choose to release it. I trust in my ability to handle difficult situations with grace and competence. My worth is not solely defined by my work, and I am more than the challenges I encounter. I take a deep breath, letting go of tension, and focus on what I can control. I am committed to my well-being, and choose to cultivate a positive and peaceful mindset. Tomorrow is a new day, filled with opportunities for growth and success. I am strong, and I can overcome any challenges that come my way.

# I Am Having A Hard Time With Mourning The Loss of A Loved One Today

Though the pain of loss is heavy, I honor the love and memories that live on in my heart. Today is a tough day, and that's okay. I allow myself to feel the emotions, acknowledge the depth of my love and connection. In this moment of grief, I am surrounded by the warmth of cherished memories. I am resilient, and each tear is a testament to the profound bond I shared. As I navigate this difficult day, I choose to be gentle with myself. Healing is a gradual process and I trust that, in time, the weight of sorrow will ease. I carry the love of my lost one within me, and their legacy will continue to inspire and comfort me.

# I Feel Challenged With Fear And Anxiety

In this moment of fear and anxiety, I choose to ground myself in the present. I am stronger than my fears, and I have the power to overcome challenges. My mind is clear, and I release the thoughts that do not serve my well-being. I breathe in calmness, exhale tension, and trust in my ability to navigate through uncertainty. I am resilient, and I have overcome obstacles before. Each breath is a step forward, and I am moving towards a place of peace. I acknowledge my feeling without judgement and I choose to focus on the positive possibilities that lie ahead. I am capable, and I trust in my strength to face whatever comes my way.

## My Emotions Have Been Challenged After Breaking Up With My Significant Other

Even in the midst of heartache, I am a resilient and valuable individual. My emotions are valid, and I allow myself to feel and heal. This breakup is a chapter in my life, not the whole story. I am not defined by this moment of pain. I choose to release what no longer serves me and embrace the opportunity for growth. I am worthy of love and happiness, and this experience is a stepping stone towards a brighter and more fulfilling future. I am healing, I am growing, and I am rediscovering the strength within myself. Each day brings me closer to a place of peace and self-love.

# I Am Heartbroken

Though my heart is heavy, it is also resilient. I honor the depth of my emotions and recognize that healing is a process. I am not alone on this journey; I have strength within me to overcome this pain. Each beat of my heart is a testament to my capacity for love and renewal. I embrace the healing energy that surrounds me, and with time, I know that my heart will mend. I am deserving of love, both from others and from myself. As I navigate through this heartbreak, I am also navigating toward a brighter and more loving future. I am strong, I am worthy, and I am on the path to healing.

# I Am Afraid To Make Mistakes

I embrace the opportunity to learn and grow. Mistakes are stepping stones on my journey, not barriers. I release the fear of making errors and instead welcome them as lessons that contribute to my wisdom. Each mistake is a chance for improvement, and I am resilient in the face of challenges. I trust in my ability to navigate throught life's uncertainties. I am not defined by my mistakes, but by my capacity to rise above them. I give myself permission to be imperfect and acknowledge that, in doing so, I am allowing space for progress and self-discovery. I am learning, evolving, and becoming a better
version of myself everyday.

## I Am Having A Hard Time Sticking To My Diet Regimin

I am more than my diet choices, and I am not defined by a single meal or day. I acknowledge that I am on a journey toward a healthier lifestyle, and its okay to have moments of flexibility. I release any guilt or judgement about not sticking to my diet today. Tomorrow is a new opportunity to make nourishing choices. I choose to focus on the progress I've made and the positive steps I will take moving forward. I am committed to my well-being, and I celebrate the balance in my journey. I am mindful of my choices, and I trust in my ability to make healthier decisions in the future. I am on a path of self-improvment, and I am proud of my efforts.

# My Financial Situation Is Challenging

In the face of financial challenges, I remain resilient and resourceful. My worth is not solely determined by my financial situation. I choose to focus on abundance rather than scarcity. I am capable of finding creative solutions to improve my financial well-being. Every challenge is an opportunity for growth and learning. I am open to receiving help and guidance when needed. I trust in my ability to manage my finances wisely, and I am committed to making positive choices for my financial future. I am not defined by my current circumstances; I am defined by my strength, resilience, and ability to overcome challenges. I believe in my capacity to create a more prosperous and secure future.

# I Disappointed Someone Today

I acknowledge the impact of my actions today, and I choose to learn and grow from this experience. I am not defined by a single moment, and I am capable of making amends. I take responsibility for my actions, and I am committed to making positive changes. Mistakes do not diminish my worth; they are opportunities for reflection and improvement. I am a work in progress, and I am open to learning from my experiences. I choose to forgive myself, and I will strive to do better in the future. My actions do not define me; my willingness to learn, grow, and make amends does. I am resilient, and I am capable of building stronger and more positive connections.

# Someone Disappointed Me Today

"I acknowledge my feelings of disappointment, and I allow myself the space to process and heal. My worth is not diminished by this moment, and I choose to focus on the lessons it brings. I am resilient, and I have the strength to move forward with grace and understanding. I release any negativity and choose to cultivate a positive mindset. I am in control of my reactions, and I choose peace over prolonged resentment. I am deserving of positive and fulfilling relationships, and I trust that my path will lead me to connections that uplift and support me. I am empowered to create my own happiness, and I release the disappointment, making room for brighter and more positive experiences ahead."

# I Feel The Need To Apologize

I acknowledge the impact of my actions, and I am brave enough to take responsibility. I am not defined by my mistakes, but by my ability to learn and grow. I choose to offer a sincere apology, recognizing the strength it takes to admit fault. I am committed to making amends and building stronger connections. My willingness to apologize reflects my integrity and commitment to positive relationships. I forgive myself and others, knowing that forgiveness is a powerful tool for healing. I am on a journey of continuous improvement, and each apology is an opportunity for greater understanding and compassion. I choose to move forward with grace and openness.

# I Didn't Receive An Apology

"I acknowledge the absence of an apology, and I release the need for external validation. I am worthy of respect and understanding, and I choose to find my peace within. I am not defined by the actions or words of others. I release any resentment and choose to focus on my own growth and well-being. I am strong and resilient, and I recognize that my worth is not dependent on external apologies. I have the power to create a positive and nurturing environment for myself. I choose to let go of what I cannot control and move forward with grace. I am deserving of kindness, and I cultivate it within myself, creating a space for healing and positivity."

# My Mental Health Feels Challenged at Times

I am resilient, and I acknowledge that it's okay to face challenges with my mental health. Each day is a new opportunity for healing and growth. I choose to treat myself with kindness and compassion during difficult moments. My mental health does not define me, and seeking support is a sign of strength. I am not alone in this journey, and I am surrounded by resources and people who care about my well-being. I give myself permission to prioritize self-care and take the necessary steps to nurture my mental health. I am strong, and I am capable of overcoming any obstacles that come my way.

# I Feel Discouraged Because I Am Not Married

My worth is not determined by my marital status. I trust that my journey is unique, and I embrace the path I am on. I am whole and complete just as I am. I release any societal pressures or expectations about my relationship status. I am deserving of love, and I trust that the right person and the right timing will align in my life. In the meantime, I focus on becoming the best version of myself and building a fulfilling life. I celebrate my independence and the opportunities for personal growth that come with it. I trust in the timing of my life and believe that everything is unfolding as it should.

# I Feel Discouraged Because I Don't Have Children

My worth is not defined by whether or not I have children. I trust in the unfolding of my life journey and recognize that every path is unique. I embrace the opportunities for self-discovery and personal growth that come with my current circumstances. I release any societal expectations or pressures, allowing myself the space to navigate my own journey. I am complete and whole as I am. I celebrate the freedom to create a life that aligns with my values and aspirations. Whether or not I have children, my life is meaningful, and I am capable of nurturing deep connections and leaving a positive impact on the world.

# I Feel Lonely

I am never truly alone; I am surrounded by love, both within and around me. I embrace the solitude as an opportunity for self-discovery and growth. I am worthy of meaningful connections, and I am open to the beauty that comes with each new relationship. I choose to nurture the existing connections in my life and to welcome new ones when the time is right. Loneliness is a temporary state, and I am actively creating a life filled with love, understanding, and joy. I appreciate my own company and find fulfillment in the present moment. I am a beacon of light, attracting positive and genuine connections into my life.

# I Miss My Family

Though miles may separate us, the love and connection I share with my family remain strong. I cherish the memories we've created and the bonds that tie us together. In moments of longing, I focus on the love that unites us, transcending any distance. I am grateful for the moments we've shared and look forward to creating more in the future. My family is always in my heart, and their love sustains me. I carry the warmth of our connections with me, finding comfort in the love that knows no boundaries. Until we reunite, I am surrounded by the love that we've built together.

# Sometimes I Don't Feel Attractive

I am more than my physical appearance. My worth goes beyond what can be seen. I recognize the unique qualities and strengths that make me who I am. Beauty is diverse, and I am a unique expression of it. I choose to focus on the aspects of myself that radiate confidence, kindness, and authenticity. True attractiveness comes from within, and I embrace the beauty that comes from a genuine and compassionate heart. I am deserving of love and appreciation just as I am. Today, I celebrate the unique and wonderful qualities that make me uniquely me."

# I Don't Feel Understood

I am a complex and unique individual, and it's okay if not everyone understands me fully. I value and understand myself, and that is what truly matters. I communicate my thoughts and feelings with clarity, and I am open to sharing more when necessary. I am patient with others as they may not fully grasp my experiences. I surround myself with those who appreciate and respect me for who I am. I am constantly evolving, and each day is an opportunity to better understand myself and be understood by others. My worth is not contingent on others' understanding, but on my ability to stay true to myself.

# Sometimes Its Challenging For Me To Concentrate

I am capable and focused. In moments of distraction, I gently bring my attention back to the task at hand. Each breath I take centers me, allowing me to concentrate with clarity. I release any tension or stress that hinders my focus. I trust in my ability to overcome distractions and stay present in this moment. I am in control of my mind, and I choose to direct my energy toward the task in front of me. With each passing moment, my concentration grows stronger. I am focused, I am capable, and I am fully present in the now.

# I Am Practicing Self Motivation

I am a powerful force, fully capable of achieving my goals. Challenges are opportunities for growth, and I tackle them with determination. I trust in my ability to overcome obstacles and stay focused on my aspirations. Each step I take is a stride toward success, and I am relentless in the pursuit of my dreams. I am motivated, I am resilient, and I am the architect of my own success. I believe in my potential, and I am energized to create a future filled with achievement and fulfillment.

# Self Love Is Priority

I am deserving of love and kindness. I embrace the unique qualities that make me who I am. My worth is not determined by external validations; I am valuable simply because I exist. I treat myself with compassion and prioritize my well-being. I celebrate the journey of self-discovery and acknowledge that I am constantly evolving. I am a source of love, and I radiate positivity to myself and others. Today, I choose to love and accept myself unconditionally.

# Today, I Hold Myself Accountable

I am accountable for my actions and choices. I embrace responsibility as a path to growth. I learn from my mistakes and celebrate my successes. Each day is an opportunity to make choices aligned with my values. I am mindful of my goals, and I take deliberate steps toward achieving them. I am in control of my decisions, and I trust in my ability to create positive change. Accountability is my strength, and I welcome it as a tool for personal and continual improvement

# I Will Not Overeat Today

I nourish my body with care and respect. I am mindful of my eating choices and listen to my body's signals. Today, I choose to eat in moderation, savoring each bite with intention. I am in control of my relationship with food, and I choose nourishment over excess. I honor my body's needs and trust in my ability to make healthy choices. Each decision I make contributes to my well-being, and I am empowered to create a positive and balanced relationship with food."

# I Choose To Be Humble Regardless Of The Situation

I approach every situation with humility and an open heart. I acknowledge the wisdom that comes from learning and recognize the value in every experience. Regardless of the circumstance, I choose to listen, learn, and grow. I release the need to be right and embrace the opportunity to gain understanding. I am humble, appreciating the lessons that humility brings. In every interaction, I contribute to a positive and harmonious environment, fostering connections built on respect and mutual learning."

# I Am Moving On From The Memories Of A Difficult Childhood

I am resilient and capable of breaking free from the shadows of my difficult childhood. I release the weight of the past and step into the light of my own potential. I am not defined by my upbringing; I am defined by the strength I carry within. Each day is a new opportunity for healing, growth, and self-discovery. I am in control of my narrative, and I choose to create a future filled with love, joy, and positive experiences. I am breaking free from the chains of the past and embracing the boundless possibilities of my own journey.

# Defeating Perfectionsim

I release the need for perfection and embrace the beauty of my imperfections. My worth is not determined by flawless achievements, but by my journey, growth, and resilience. I celebrate progress over perfection, understanding that mistakes are stepping stones to success. I am free from the shackles of perfectionism, and I welcome the joy that comes from embracing the authenticity of who I am. Today, I choose self-compassion, recognizing that I am enough just as I am. I am on a journey of continual improvement, and each step forward is a victory.

# Afraid of Commitment

I release my fear of commitment and embrace the opportunities that come with deep connections. I trust in my ability to navigate and grow within committed relationships. Each step I take towards commitment is a step towards personal and relational growth. I am deserving of love and security, and I open myself to the richness that committed connections can bring. I release the anxiety surrounding commitment, knowing that it is a path towards fulfillment and shared experiences. I am strong, capable, and ready to embrace the beauty that commitment can bring to my life.

# I Acknowledge The Need For Self Control

I am in control of my choices and actions. I embrace the power of self-control, making decisions that align with my goals and values. I trust in my ability to resist impulses that do not serve my well-being. Each moment of self-control is a step toward personal growth and success. I am mindful of my actions, and I choose to act in ways that honor my truest self. I am strong, focused, and capable of making choices that contribute to my overall well-being. With each display of self-control, I empower myself to live a life aligned with my aspirations.

# I Am Enough

I am enough just as I am. My worth is not determined by external validations or expectations. I embrace my imperfections as unique qualities that make me who I am. I am worthy of love, acceptance, and all the good things life has to offer. My journey is a constant evolution, and each step I take adds to my completeness. I release self-doubt and embrace the truth that I am deserving of happiness and fulfillment. Today, I affirm my worthiness, acknowledging that I am more than enough.

# Seeking Validation

I am secure in my own worth, and I do not need external validation to define my value. I recognize the strength that lies within me and trust in my capabilities. I am proud of my achievements and choices, and I validate myself. The opinions of others do not determine my worth. I am on a journey of self-discovery, and I am confident in the person I am becoming. Today, I affirm my own worth and acknowledge the inherent value I bring to every aspect of my life.

# I Take Responsibility For My Actions

I take full responsibility for my actions, acknowledging the impact they may have had. I am committed to learning from my mistakes and using them as stepping stones toward growth. Today, I choose accountability as a path to personal development. I am empowered to make amends and move forward with wisdom and integrity. Each moment of responsibility is an opportunity for positive change, and I am capable of creating a better version of myself through mindful actions and thoughtful choices.

# Dealing With Hurt Feelings

I acknowledge my hurt feelings, and I give myself the compassion I deserve. I am allowed to feel, and my emotions are valid. In this moment of pain, I choose to nurture my wounded heart with kindness and understanding. I release negativity and open myself to healing and growth. I am resilient, and I trust that, with time, my hurt feelings will transform into strength and wisdom. I am in control of my emotional well-being, and I choose to focus on the positive aspects of my life. Today, I give myself the space and grace to heal and move forward with a heart full of resilience and hope.

# It Wasn't My Best Performance

I acknowledge that today's performance wasn't my best, and that's okay. My worth is not solely determined by a single moment. I am a work in progress, and I recognize the opportunity for growth in every experience. I choose to learn from this, accepting it as a step in my journey toward improvement. I release perfectionism and embrace the beauty of imperfection. I am resilient, and I trust that my commitment to learning and evolving will lead me to greater success in the future. Today's performance is just one chapter in my story, and I am the author of a narrative filled with growth, learning, and eventual triumph.

*live laugh love*

# Farewell Stinking Thinking

I release the negative thoughts that hold me back. I am in control of my mindset, and I choose positivity. I let go of self-doubt and embrace self-empowerment. My thoughts create my reality, and I choose to focus on the good. I am capable, worthy, and deserving of success. Today, I break free from stinking thinking, and I welcome a mindset of possibility and optimism. I am the architect of my thoughts, and I choose to build a foundation of positivity, resilience, and growth.

# Goodbye Self Sabotage

I am letting go of self-sabotage and embracing a path of self-love and growth. I release the patterns that no longer serve me and open myself to positive change. I am deserving of success, happiness, and fulfillment. Today, I choose to break free from self-sabotaging behaviors and embrace the limitless potential within me. I am the captain of my ship, navigating toward a future filled with self-empowerment and success. Goodbye, self-sabotage; hello, positive transformation.

# Taking Care Of Me

I prioritize self-care and honor my well-being. In taking care of myself, I nurture my mind, body, and spirit. I am deserving of the love and attention I give to others. Today, I affirm my commitment to self-love and self-care. I listen to my needs and respond with kindness. Each act of self-care is a celebration of my worth, and I embrace the journey to becoming the best version of myself. I am important, and I choose to invest in my health and happiness.

# Feeling Devalued

I am valuable, deserving of respect, love, and consideration. My worth is not determined by others' opinions or actions. I recognize the strength within me, and I choose to honor and uplift myself. I release any negative energy that attempts to diminish my value. I am a unique and valuable individual, and I stand tall in my worth. Today, I affirm my own significance and embrace the inherent value that resides within me.

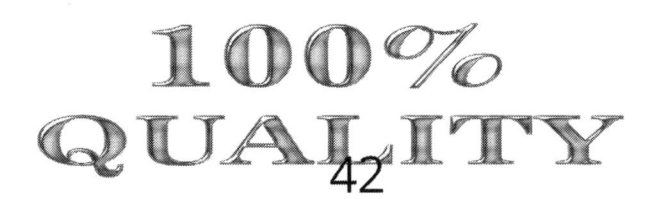

100% QUALITY

# I Am Worthy Of Appreciation

I am worthy of appreciation, and my contributions have value. Even if others may not express it, I acknowledge the impact of my efforts. I celebrate my own accomplishments and recognize the value I bring to the table. I don't seek external validation to feel my worth; I carry it within me. Today, I affirm my own significance, and I take pride in the work I do. I am deserving of appreciation, and I choose to honor and recognize my own efforts.

# I Am Thankful

I am grateful for the abundance in my life. Today, I choose to focus on the positive and express gratitude for both the big and small blessings. I appreciate the opportunities for growth and the joy that surrounds me. Gratitude is my guiding light, and I am thankful for the richness that each moment brings. I am open to receiving and giving thanks, creating a cycle of positivity in my life. Today and every day, I choose to embrace a heart full of gratitude.

BE YE
GRATEFUL

# I Am Blessed

I am blessed with abundance and grace in every aspect of my life. I acknowledge the blessings that flow into my life daily, both seen and unseen. I am open to receiving the gifts that come my way and appreciate the beauty that surrounds me. Today, I am grateful for the many blessings that enrich my journey. I carry a heart full of gratitude, recognizing the divine abundance that fills my life. I am blessed, and I choose to embrace the blessings that unfold in every moment.

# Moving Past Feelings Of Betrayal

I release the pain of betrayal and choose to move forward with strength and grace. I am not defined by the actions of others, and I am in control of my own healing. Today, I affirm my resilience and choose to focus on my well-being. I release resentment and embrace the freedom that comes with forgiveness. I am stronger than the hurt, and I am moving towards a future filled with trust, peace, and authenticity. I am in control of my narrative, and I choose to create a positive and empowered story for myself.

# Loss Of A Bestfriend

I acknowledge the pain of losing a best friend, and I give myself the compassion to grieve. In this moment of loss, I choose to remember the joy and meaningful connections we shared. I release the heaviness of the goodbye and embrace the lessons and love that friendship brought into my life. Though the chapter has ended, I trust in new beginnings and the potential for new connections. I am resilient, and my heart is open to the beauty of future friendships. I carry the positive memories with me, and I am grateful for the growth and experiences we shared.

**PEACE**

# **Parenthood Is A Joyful Journey**

Parenting is a joyful journey, filled with moments of love, laughter, and connection. I embrace the joy that parenthood brings into my life. Each day is an opportunity to witness the wonder of my child's growth and to share in the joy of their discoveries. I am grateful for the love and warmth that permeates our home. Today and every day, I choose to celebrate the joyous moments of parenthood and to savor the precious memories we create together.

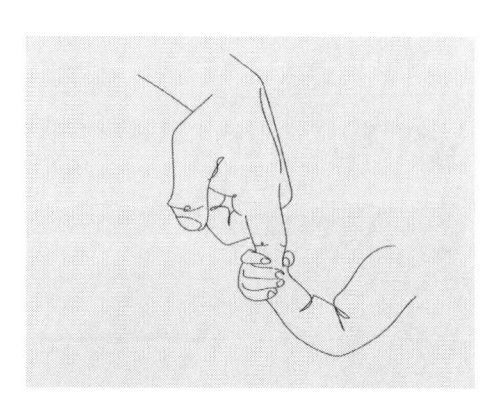

# Parenting Is Challenging

Parenting is a challenging yet rewarding journey, and I am resilient in the face of difficulties. I trust in my ability to navigate the complexities of parenthood with patience and love. Challenges are opportunities for growth, and I am constantly learning and evolving. I release the need for perfection and embrace the imperfections that make our journey unique. I am a capable and loving parent, and I am supported by the strength that comes from facing challenges head-on. Each day, I choose to find joy in the small victories and appreciate the lessons that parenthood teaches me.

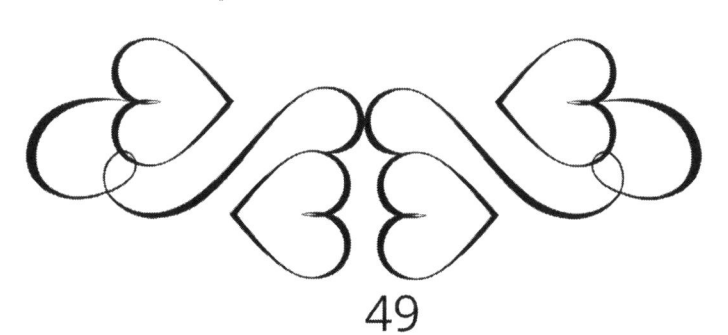

## I Believe That I Will Be Successful In All That I Do

I am a magnet for success, and I believe in my ability to achieve greatness in all aspects of my life. My confidence is unwavering, and I attract positive opportunities with my positive mindset. I am resilient in the face of challenges, and I see setbacks as stepping stones to success. Today and every day, I affirm that success is my natural state, and I am open to the abundance that flows into my life. I am capable, I am determined, and I am on the path to achieving my goals and dreams.

*Be You ♥ ♥ Be True Just Be ♥*

Made in United States
Orlando, FL
17 June 2024